Robert Oppenheimer

Biography for kids and beginners

Author: Alia B

ALIAREDA © 2023

book plan

Introduction

Explore the amazing world of Robert Oppenheimer, a scientist whose groundbreaking work changed the course of history for good. In this interesting biography, both kids and adults can learn about the life and accomplishments of the man who came up with the idea for the atomic bomb.

Follow Oppenheimer's life from his childhood as a curious and inquisitive boy to his time at Harvard and the University of Cambridge, where he got a good education. He became well-known as a brilliant physicist who did groundbreaking work in quantum mechanics and nuclear physics.

This biography shows the ups and downs of Oppenheimer's life, from his important role as head of the top-secret

Manhattan Project during World War II to the moral questions he had to think about when the destructive power of the atomic bomb became a reality.

But Oppenheimer wasn't just a scientist. Learn more about his personal life to understand how complex he was as a person. Find out why he loves books, how much he cares about education, and why he wants scientific research to be open and collaborative.

This biography is a fascinating look at Oppenheimer's contributions, controversies, and lasting legacy. It is great for both young people who want to learn about scientific pioneers and adults who want to know everything about his life. Find out about the fascinating life of Robert Oppenheimer, a man whose scientific genius and moral thoughts helped shape the world we live in today.

1. Lessons Learned from Robert Oppenheimer

In this chapter, we'll look at some important lessons that kids can learn from Robert Oppenheimer's life and work. Oppenheimer was an American physicist who was very important in making the atomic bomb during World War II. Even though his story is complicated, we can learn some important lessons from it.

Lesson 1: Pursue knowledge with curiosity and passion

Robert Oppenheimer was very interested in learning and always wanted to know more. He was a great example of the idea that knowledge is a powerful tool and should always be pursued with passion. Children can learn from him that they should never stop wanting to learn and that trying out new things and ideas can lead to great things.

Lesson 2: Embrace diversity and collaborate

Oppenheimer knew how important it was to work together and how important it was to have different ideas in order to do great things. In order to make the atomic bomb, the Manhattan Project brought together scientists from many different fields. Children can learn from Oppenheimer that they can accomplish more and come up with new ways to solve problems if they work with people who have different points of view.

Lesson 3: Understand the consequences of actions

Oppenheimer's work on the atomic bomb was certainly a scientific achievement, but he also had to deal with moral questions about the effects of what he had made. Children can learn how important it is to think about what might happen before taking action and making good decisions.

This lesson teaches kids to think about the moral effects of their choices.

Lesson 4: Learn from mistakes and accept responsibility

After seeing the terrible effects of the atomic bomb, people said that Oppenheimer shouldn't have been involved in the project. Children can learn how important it is to learn from their mistakes, take responsibility for what they did, and work hard to make things right. This lesson tells kids to take responsibility for their actions and try to grow and get better.

Lesson 5: Stand up for what is right

After the war, Oppenheimer talked about how worried he was about the spread of nuclear weapons. He called for more control and for the world to stop making nuclear weapons. Children can learn from him to stand up for what they think is right, even when it's hard, and to use their voices to make the world a better place. This lesson shows kids how important it is to be involved, well-informed citizens who work for good change.

The story of Robert Oppenheimer's life can give kids ideas and teach them important lessons. Children can follow in Oppenheimer's footsteps and help make the world a better place by being curious, working with others, understanding consequences, admitting when they're wrong, and standing up for what's right.

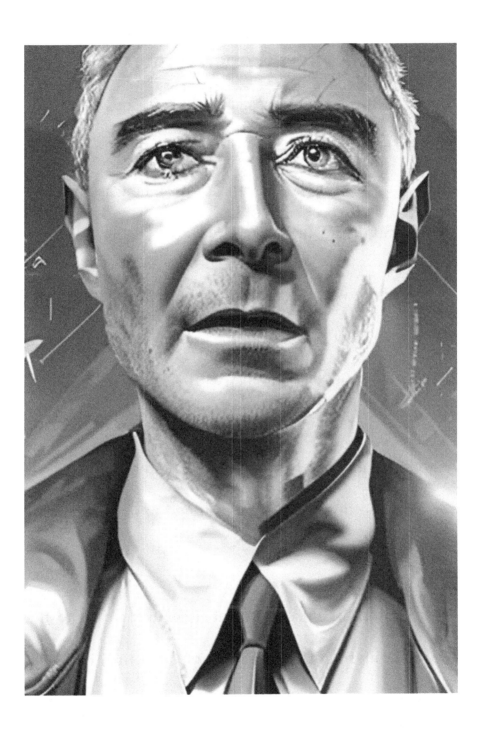

2. Who is Robert Oppenheimer?

American theoretical physicist and professor Robert Oppenheimer is best known for his work on the atomic bomb during World War II. On April 22, 1904, he was born to a wealthy family in New York City.

Oppenheimer was very smart from a young age and went to school in New York City at the Ethical Culture Fieldston School. He then went to Harvard University to study physics and graduated with honors at the age of 18. Then he went to Germany to get his Ph.D. in physics at the University of Gottingen, where he studied under the famous physicist Max Born.

After getting his Ph.D., Oppenheimer went back to the U.S. and taught at the University of California, Berkeley. He became known quickly as a smart and creative physicist, especially for his groundbreaking work on quantum theory. Oppenheimer made important contributions to theoretical physics, especially in the area of quantum mechanics.

During World War II, Oppenheimer was asked to join the secret Manhattan Project, whose goal was to make an atomic bomb. He was put in charge of the scientists and engineers working on the design and development of the bomb at the Los Alamos Laboratory in New Mexico.

Oppenheimer was a key part of the success of the Manhattan Project. He oversaw the testing and eventual use of the atomic bombs that were dropped on the Japanese cities of Hiroshima and Nagasaki in August 1945. In the end, Japan gave up and World War II was over because of the bombings.

But Oppenheimer's work on the project to make an atomic

bomb had a big effect on him as a person. After seeing how powerful the bomb was and how bad its effects were, he became a strong supporter of nuclear disarmament and spoke out against making and using more atomic weapons.

Oppenheimer taught at the Institute for Advanced Study in Princeton, New Jersey, after the war. He kept working on theoretical physics research and made important contributions in many areas. As a science advisor to the government, Oppenheimer also had a big impact on how science and education were handled in the United States.

During the McCarthy era, in the early 1950s, Oppenheimer's political views and connections came under close scrutiny. He was told that he was a threat to security and liked communism. Oppenheimer's security clearance was taken away at a very controversial hearing. This meant that he could no longer advise the government and hurt his reputation in the scientific community.

Even though this was a setback, Oppenheimer kept doing research and teaching until 1966, when he retired. During his career, he won a lot of awards and honors, like the Enrico Fermi Award and the National Medal of Science.

Robert Oppenheimer died at the age of 62 on February 18, 1967. He is remembered as one of the smartest people of his time and for his contradictory role in making the atomic bomb and then working for the end of nuclear weapons.

3. The Curious Mind of Young Robert Oppenheimer

Robert Oppenheimer was born in New York City on April 22, 1904. His parents put a lot of value on education and learning. Robert was always interested in what was going on around him, even when he was very young. This chapter looks at Robert's formative years as a child. It shows how smart he was and shows the seeds of his future brilliance.

Since Robert grew up in a wealthy family, he had access to a huge number of books, which he eagerly read. Even before he could read, he would spend hours turning the pages of books, looking at the pictures, and making up his own stories. By the time he was three, Robert already knew how to read, and he was often found with his nose in a hard-to-understand book about science or philosophy.

Robert's natural curiosity was fed by family trips to museums, where he would eagerly look at every exhibit and ask his parents a million questions about the wonders of the world. His parents would answer all of his questions patiently, no matter how hard or complicated they were.

Robert's ability to remember a lot of information was one of the things that made him stand out as a child. He seemed to have a photographic memory because he could easily remember and remember a lot of facts, numbers, and stories. Because of this talent, his parents and teachers saw that he had a lot of potential and put him in a more difficult school when he was nine years old.

Robert's desire to learn went far beyond what was taught in school. He had a strong interest in the arts and would often spend hours at museums and at musical performances. He also loved poetry and writing, which was clear from the fact that he wrote his own verses when he was young. These artistic pursuits gave him a deeper understanding of the world and helped him see it from many different angles.

Even though Robert was smart when he was young, he ran into some problems. Like many kids, he had trouble making friends and often didn't feel like he fit in with his peers. His hunger for knowledge and large vocabulary set him apart from his classmates, making him feel alone. But Robert didn't give up because of these problems. Instead, they pushed him to study harder and find comfort in the worlds of science and literature.

Robert's parents knew it was important to help him develop his special skills, so they gave him everything they could. They tried to get him to do things outside of school, like going to science lectures and joining local science clubs. He was able to talk to people with similar interests, which gave him a sense of belonging and intellectual camaraderie.

As Robert got closer to his teenage years, it became clear that the things he did as a child were making him into a remarkable person with a lot of potential to do great things. The way he could think critically, how curious he was, and how hard he tried to learn set the stage for his future work and made him the brilliant scientist he would become.

This chapter captures the essence of young Robert Oppenheimer's formative years by showing his insatiable curiosity, amazing skills, and the supportive environment that helped him grow intellectually. It hints at Robert's bright future and the important role he would play in shaping world history in the future.

4. The Enigmatic Personal Life of Robert Oppenheimer

During World War II, Robert Oppenheimer was a very smart scientist who was a key figure in making the atomic bomb. But his personal life was just as mysterious and interesting as his scientific work. This chapter looks at Oppenheimer's relationships, interests, and struggles.

Oppenheimer was born on April 22, 1904, in New York City. He grew up in a wealthy and intellectually stimulating home. Julius Oppenheimer's father was a successful German immigrant who ran a business that brought in textiles. Ella Friedman, his mother, came from a wealthy family with ties to the arts. Oppenheimer was very interested in many things from a young age, including science, literature, and philosophy.

Oppenheimer did a lot of good work in school. He got his

bachelor's degree from Harvard University, where he was one of the smartest students in the department of theoretical physics. Later, he got his PhD at Germany's University of Gottingen, where he worked with famous physicists like Max Born and Werner Heisenberg. These things changed the way he thought about science and set the stage for his groundbreaking contributions to physics.

Oppenheimer's personal life was full of strong feelings and complicated relationships. In 1929, he married his first wife, an artist and activist named Katherine Puening Harrison. But the marriage didn't last long, and in 1939 they split up. Even though they were no longer together, they stayed friends for the rest of their lives.

After he got divorced, Oppenheimer adopted a bohemian way of life and got involved in the lively social and cultural scenes of Berkeley, California, and New Mexico. He hung out with artists, thinkers, and activists, which gave him a broader view of the world and let him explore his own creative side. This time in his life had a big impact on how he got involved in left-wing political movements later on.

During the Red Scare of the 1940s and 1950s, people were interested in Oppenheimer's left-leaning political views. He had been involved with a number of left-wing groups and knew some communists. The government was worried about his loyalty, so they did a number of investigations that led to his security clearance being taken away in 1954.

After the war was over, Oppenheimer went back to school. He was put in charge of the Institute for Advanced Study in Princeton, where he helped young physicists who wanted to learn more. Even though his personal life was controversial, his intelligence and contributions to science were highly regarded, and he was still a well-known figure in the scientific world.

In the last part of his life, Oppenheimer stayed out of the public eye for the most part. He had problems with his health, like throat cancer, which killed him on February 18, 1967. Even though his personal life was full of problems, Oppenheimer's contributions to science and his key role in making the atomic bomb are still important parts of human history.

Robert Oppenheimer's personal life was complicated by his relationships, his political views, and the problems of his time. Understanding the different parts of his personal life helps us figure out the genius mind that changed the course of human history for good.

5. The Professional Career of Robert Oppenheimer

The seeds of Robert Oppenheimer's future work life were planted when he was young. Oppenheimer was born on April 22, 1904, in New York City. He grew up in a wealthy and intellectually stimulating home. His father, Julius Oppenheimer, came from Germany and set up a successful business importing textiles. Ella Friedman was his mother, and she was from Baltimore. She loved art and literature very much. Both of Robert's parents knew he was very smart and helped him pursue his interests from a young age.

When Oppenheimer went to Harvard University in 1922, it was clear that he was going to have a career in science. He studied chemistry, philosophy, and literature at Harvard, among other things. But it was Percy Bridgman's physics class that sparked his interest and got him started on the path to becoming a physicist. Oppenheimer wanted to learn more, so he got a Ph.D. in physics at the University of Gottingen, where he was taught by the famous Max Born. After getting his PhD in 1927, Oppenheimer moved back to the United States and started a successful career. He was drawn to theoretical physics and became an expert in quantum mechanics and how subatomic particles behave. His intelligence and creativity, along with his ability to teach and work well with others, led to many scientific advances.

In 1939, Oppenheimer and one of his students, George Volkoff, published a seminal paper in which they proposed the existence of neutron stars. This was his most important contribution. This ground-breaking work made it possible to study these dense objects in space and opened up a whole new area of astrophysics. Some of his other important papers were about spectroscopy, nuclear physics, and quantum theory, among other things.

In the early 1940s, when he was put in charge of the scientific side of the Manhattan Project, Oppenheimer's career took a big turn. During World War II, this top-secret US government project was meant to help make an atomic bomb. Oppenheimer's brilliant mind, leadership skills, and ability to work well with scientists from different fields were key to the success of the project.

Oppenheimer was in charge of the Los Alamos Laboratory, which was where some of the best scientists of the time worked together. Oppenheimer was a great organizer, and he insisted on keeping conversations open and encouraging people to work together. This made it possible for ground-breaking discoveries to be made. The first atomic bomb, code-named Trinity, was successfully tested on July 16, 1945. This event changed the world for good.

After World War II ended, Oppenheimer became more involved in making science policy. He used to focus on research and academia, but after the war was over, he shifted his attention to science policy. As a government advisor, he was asked a lot of questions about nuclear policy and controlling nuclear arms. This was especially true for the newly formed Atomic Energy Commission.

But Oppenheimer's career took an unexpected turn in 1954, when the Atomic Energy Commission held a security hearing for him because communist sympathizers said he had worked with them. Even though he had helped the country, his security clearance was taken away. This event had a big effect on Oppenheimer. It caused him to quit his scientific advisory jobs and change his goals for his career.

Even though the security hearing was a setback, Robert Oppenheimer continued to have an impact on science. He went back to teaching and became the director of Princeton University's Institute for Advanced Study in 1947. He stayed in that job until 1966. During this time, Oppenheimer taught and inspired a new generation of physicists, leaving an indelible mark on the field. Robert Oppenheimer's career showed how smart he was, how creative he could be, and how dedicated he was to making scientific knowledge better. Even though his role in making atomic weapons was controversial, it is still important in history. Above all, Oppenheimer was one of the most important scientists of the 20th century because of his scientific achievements and the huge impact he had as a teacher and mentor.

6. The Unconventional Teaching Career of Robert Oppenheimer

As Robert Oppenheimer's scientific achievements and leadership in the Manhattan Project got more attention, he found himself at a crossroads. Even though he still had a lot of work to do as a physicist, he had a strong desire to teach and shape the minds of people who would come after him. Robert Oppenheimer's teaching career was unique because of his charisma, intelligence, and desire to encourage students to think critically.

After World War II was over, Oppenheimer had to deal with the moral problems that came with the use of atomic weapons. He questioned how scientific knowledge should be used responsibly and worked to help people learn more about the effects of science through education. Oppenheimer was sure that a well-informed society was the only way to keep future disasters from happening.

In 1947, Oppenheimer became a physics professor at the University of California, Berkeley, which was a big deal at the time. His lectures had an electric energy that kept students from many different backgrounds interested. Oppenheimer's classes were full of lively discussions in which he pushed his students to question well-known scientific theories and look at things from different points of view.

Robert Oppenheimer's lessons were about more than just physics. He knew how important it was to learn from different fields, so he used ideas from philosophy, literature, and history in his lectures. Oppenheimer told students to think about the ethical aspects of scientific progress and how their discoveries would affect society.

Oppenheimer thought that his job as a teacher was not just to pass on information, but also to help guide and train scientists of the future. By creating an environment where people were intellectually curious and worked together, he helped many talented physicists start their careers. Many of his students became well-known scientists and carried on Oppenheimer's idea that science should move forward in a responsible way.

Even though he did good work in academia, Oppenheimer's career was closely watched by politicians during the McCarthy era. The development of the atomic bomb led to fears that Oppenheimer was a communist, so the government started looking into his loyalty. His teaching career was affected by this rough time, but he never stopped caring about teaching.

Oppenheimer's security clearance was taken away in 1954 because he was linked to people who were thought to be communists. This setback had a big effect on both his teaching job and his scientific research. But his work as a teacher lived on, teaching generations of students to think critically and think about how scientific progress affects ethics.

Oppenheimer quit teaching at the University of California, Berkeley, in 1966, which was the end of his unusual teaching career. But he never stopped caring about education. He stayed involved in academic circles, going to conferences and giving guest lectures. Oppenheimer was dedicated to promoting a well-rounded education that included more than just science until he died in 1967.

In the end, Robert Oppenheimer's teaching career was defined by his constant desire to teach future scientists a sense of responsibility and ethics. His unconventional way of teaching, which included mixing science and philosophy and getting students to talk about anything they wanted, made sure that his influence went far beyond the classroom. Robert Oppenheimer's legacy as a teacher shows how important teachers are in shaping the minds of the next generation.

7. The Expanding Horizons of Scientific Work

After World War II, scientific research and development became more important than ever. Governments all over the world knew that technological advances, especially in the field of nuclear physics, could be dangerous and powerful. Robert Oppenheimer stands out among the many great scientists who helped this field grow and develop because of his ground-breaking work and visionary ideas. This chapter talks about Oppenheimer's early work and the amazing path he took to become one of the most important people in the history of modern science.

Oppenheimer was born in New York City on April 22, 1904. He loved science from a young age. His parents, Julius and Ella Oppenheimer, saw how smart he was and encouraged his interest in learning. Even though he had problems in his own life, like when his mother died of colon cancer when he was still a young teen, Oppenheimer kept studying.

After getting his bachelor's degree in physics at Harvard, Oppenheimer went to Germany to get his Ph.D. at the University of Gottingen, which was a center for scientific research at the time. During his time at Gottingen, Oppenheimer worked closely with well-known physicists like Max Born and Wolfgang Pauli, who helped him learn more about quantum mechanics. His ground-breaking research on how subatomic particles behave, especially the properties of electrons and positrons, made a big impression on the scientific community and made him known as a strong theoretical physicist.

Leading the race to build the bomb, the Manhattan Project As World War II got closer, scientists and the American government were interested in Oppenheimer's knowledge of quantum physics. The U.S. government set up the top-secret Manhattan Project to make atomic weapons because they could be used to make a weapon with power that had never been seen before. Oppenheimer was hired to lead the project's scientific work because he was known as a brilliant physicist.

Under Oppenheimer's direction, an elite team of scientists and engineers pushed the limits of what was known at the time. They worked day and night to figure out how to use the energy locked up in the nucleus of an atom. Oppenheimer's leadership was so far-sighted that it not only inspired his team but also led to some of the most important discoveries ever made. He worked with Enrico Fermi to make the first nuclear reactor, which showed that nuclear energy could be released in a controlled way.

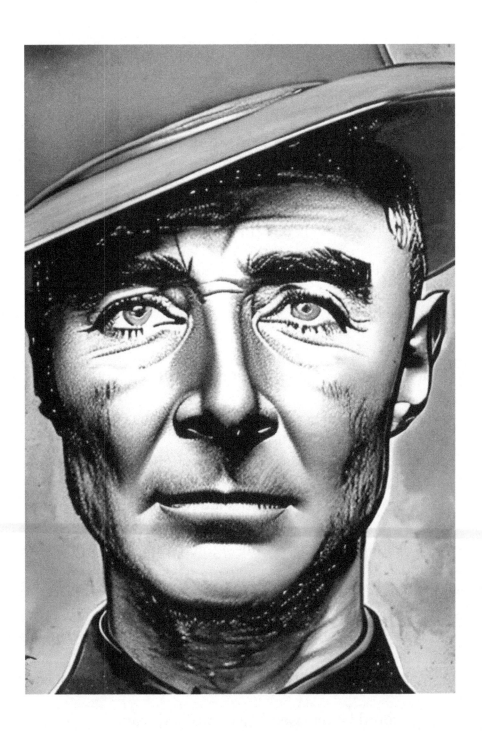

As the Manhattan Project was almost done, Oppenheimer was in charge of putting together the Trinity Test, which was the first time a nuclear device went off successfully. It happened in the New Mexico desert in July 1945. When Oppenheimer saw how much power the bomb released, he was reminded of a famous quote from the Bhagavad Gita: "Now I have become Death, the destroyer of worlds."

The success of the test was a turning point in the history of science, because it showed the world how destructive atomic weapons could be. Oppenheimer's work on the Manhattan Project and his role in bringing about the atomic age made him a well-known figure after World War II ended. Some people admired him, while others hated him.

Robert Oppenheimer's work in science changed the course of history, especially in the fields of quantum physics and nuclear research. His groundbreaking work on atomic energy, which led to the Manhattan Project, shows how smart and good at leading he was. Even though he helped make the world's first atomic bomb, which was hard on his conscience, Oppenheimer spent the rest of his career working to improve international scientific cooperation and stop the spread of weapons of mass destruction. So, his scientific work showed both the promise and the dangers of human creativity. It was a constant reminder that scientists have a responsibility to use their discoveries for the good of humanity.

8. The Manhattan Project and Robert Oppenheimer

In the spring of 1942, a secret group was set up and given the code name "The Manhattan Project." The goal of this project was to make an atomic bomb, and it would change the course of human history for all time. J. Robert Oppenheimer, a smart and complicated physicist, was in charge of this ambitious project.

Oppenheimer was born into a wealthy and smart family in New York City in 1904. Early on, he was interested in science, and in 1927, he got his Ph.D. in physics from Harvard University. Oppenheimer quickly rose to the top of the scientific world thanks to his intelligence and amazing memory.

Oppenheimer was put in charge of the scientific side of the Manhattan Project in 1942. His job was to be in charge of a group of scientists and watch over their work on the atomic bomb. Some people were upset about Oppenheimer's appointment because he was a left-leaning politician who had worked with other left-wing activists in the past. Still, he was the best person for the job because of his great scientific achievements and deep understanding of theoretical physics.

Oppenheimer moved to Los Alamos, a remote town in New Mexico, soon after he was hired. This place would become the main lab for atomic research and the place where the atomic bomb was first made. Oppenheimer was in charge of putting together a team of smart scientists from all over the world. Many of them were European scientists who had fled Nazi Germany. Together, they worked hard to figure out how to make an atomic weapon using science and engineering.

The US government gave the Manhattan Project a lot of money and resources. The main goal of the project was to make a nuclear bomb, which they called "The Gadget." Oppenheimer was a key part of getting the scientists and engineers at Los Alamos to work together. His ability to put together complicated scientific ideas and motivate his team was key to the success of the project.

The most important step in making "The Gadget" came in July 1945, after years of hard work researching and exper-imenting. The Trinity test, which was a secret explosion of an atomic bomb, took place in the desert of New Mexico. When he saw the explosion, Oppenheimer, who was known for his poetic sense, famously quoted the Bhagavad Gita and said, "Now I have become Death, the destroyer of worlds." The success of the test was the first proof that an atomic bomb could be used as a powerful weapon.

After the Trinity test, Oppenheimer and his team could see that the atomic bomb could end the war. In August 1945, the United States bombed the Japanese cities of Hiroshima and Nagasaki with atomic bombs. Even though these bombings did bring about Japan's surrender, they also left Oppenheimer with difficult moral questions that he would have to think about for the rest of his life.

After the war, Oppenheimer became one of the most important scientists in the world because of his work on the Manhattan Project. But his political views were on the left, he was friends with communists, and he spoke out against making the hydrogen bomb. This led to a controversial security clearance hearing in 1954. Even though most scientists agreed with him, Oppenheimer's security clearance was taken away. This meant that he could no longer influence government-funded scientific research.

Some of the best scientists of the time worked together on the Manhattan Project to solve a problem that had never been faced before. It was a huge project that changed war, politics, and the course of human history for all time. Robert Oppenheimer's contributions to this project were huge, and in the end, they left an indelible mark on the world and showed how hard it is to do science when there are moral questions.

9. The Birthplace of the Atomic Bomb: Los Alamos and Robert Oppenheimer

Los Alamos is a secretive town in New Mexico. It is in the middle of a big desert and rough mountains. The world didn't know about this unremarkable place until the atomic bomb was invented there. The atomic bomb is the most powerful weapon ever made. And the mysterious Robert Oppenheimer, whose life and work would change the course of history for all time, was in charge of this groundbreaking project.

Many people call Robert Oppenheimer the "father of the atomic bomb" because he helped start the Manhattan Project, a top-secret research and development program that was meant to make an atomic weapon. Oppenheimer was born on April 22, 1904, in New York City. He was smart from a young age. He did well in school, especially in physics, and went on to get his higher education at Harvard and Cambridge, both of which are well-known.

After he finished school, Oppenheimer became known as a well-known theoretical physicist. He made important changes to the field, especially in the areas of quantum mechanics and spectroscopy. But in the early 1940s, when he was put in charge of the Los Alamos Laboratory, the center of the Manhattan Project, his life changed in a big way.

Once a remote place surrounded by mesas and canyons, Los Alamos became the hub of atomic research in the United States. Oppenheimer was in charge of a group of scientists, engineers, and technicians in this secret place. Their mission was kept secret, and all they wanted to do was make an unimaginable weapon that could end World War II.

The village itself was turned into a very safe place where nosy people couldn't see in. Los Alamos became its own world, with armed guards, barbed wire fences, and strict identity checks. As smart scientists from all over the world moved to this remote outpost, the town's population grew quickly.

Oppenheimer led in a way that was both brave and careful. He encouraged people to work together and created a place where scientists could ask lots of questions. Scientists at Los Alamos worked hard because they knew they had a huge amount of responsibility on their shoulders. They worked day and night, faced tough problems, and pushed the limits of science to find out what atomic physics was all about.

During this time, Oppenheimer's charisma and intelligence brought together a diverse group of scientists to work toward a common goal. He made an environment that encouraged open conversations, let people share their ideas, and pushed the limits of what scientists knew at the time.

But Oppenheimer had more than just a job as a scientific director at Los Alamos. He was very interested in every part of the project, from the physics to the moral questions that would come up if such a powerful weapon were used. Oppenheimer often thought about the terrible things that would happen if the bomb were ever used.

As the days turned into months and the months turned into years, the scientists at Los Alamos worked hard and ran into a lot of problems. They did a lot of test explosions to improve the design and figure out how powerful the bomb was going to be.

After many years of work, the first atomic bomb was finally set off in the deserts of New Mexico on July 16, 1945. The successful Trinity test marked the beginning of a new time in human history. The world had seen the birth of the ultimate weapon, one that would change the way wars and politics are done forever.

For Oppenheimer, the test made him feel scared and amazed all at once. As he looked at the blinding light and felt the force of the explosion, he said the famous words from the ancient Indian book Bhagavad Gita: "Now I have become Death, the destroyer of worlds." These words would always come back to him and remind him of how much power he had helped make.

Los Alamos and Robert Oppenheimer had a huge impact

on how the 20th century turned out. Even though their work was driven by the urgent needs of war, it set off a race around the world to harness the power of the atom. The things that happened in this desert town in the middle of nowhere changed the future of science, war, and humanity itself.

10. The Trinity of Robert Oppenheimer

Robert Oppenheimer looked out at the vast New Mexico desert as the sun blazed above him. On July 16, 1945, he was at the Trinity test site, where a very important thing was made. Oppenheimer stood there, feeling anxious and excited at the same time. He knew that the Trinity test would change the course of human history forever.

Trinity was the code name for the first time an atomic bomb went off. As the head of the Los Alamos Laboratory, Oppenheimer had helped make this great scientific achievement possible. The atomic bomb was made with a huge amount of help from scientists and the military, but Oppenheimer's vision and leadership were the most important parts of the project.

Oppenheimer's mind was full of doubts in the days before the Trinity test. The fact that this thing had so much power weighed heavily on him. He thought about what it would mean for the world and for morality to let loose such a destructive force. Oppenheimer knew that he had become a key part of the chain of fate for all people, with the power to change not only the outcome of the war but also the very fabric of civilization.

As the clock moved closer to midnight, Oppenheimer took a deep breath and tried to deal with the huge amount of responsibility he was carrying. The Trinity test was both the end of years of hard work and the start of an age of destruction that has never been seen before. Oppenheimer had a lot of different feelings, but they all added up to a kind of "trinity": fear, excitement, and a deep-seated desire to protect people from the destructive power of what he had made.

The desert was filled with the sound of the countdown.

The scientists were on the edge of their seats as the bomb let out its strange energy. In a matter of seconds, a huge mushroom cloud rose up over the landscape. Its eerie beauty hid the horror of how it was made. Oppenheimer stood there, amazed and saddened, as the world's most terrible weapon was made.

As the dust settled and silence fell over the barren landscape, it hit Oppenheimer hard that he had changed the course of history in a big way. His fear of the future, his excitement about the possibilities his creation offered, and his deep regret for giving the world so much power grew stronger.

The Trinity test was the start of the atomic age. It changed the way people think about science, war, and the balance of power for good. Oppenheimer would always have to deal with the weight of his trinity. He became a supporter of limiting the number of weapons in the world and a voice of caution in the midst of war. He once made a famous quote from Hindu scripture after seeing the Trinity test. He said, "Now I have become Death, the destroyer of worlds." These words summed up the pain and responsibility that had come to define Robert Oppenheimer.

In the years that followed, Oppenheimer's three feelings forced him to face the long-term effects of what he had made. He worked hard to make sure that nuclear weapons were never used again, and he became a strong supporter of using nuclear energy for peaceful purposes. As Oppenheimer devoted himself to saving humanity, the Trinity went from being a burden to being a force for change.

Oppenheimer's name would always be linked to the Trinity test. He had helped make the most destructive force possible, but his three emotions turned him into a guardian of balance who tried to stop that power from being released on the world. His story would always be linked to the creation of the atomic bomb, making him a symbol of the complicated relationship between scientific progress and moral responsibility.

11. The Postwar Activities of Robert Oppenheimer

Robert Oppenheimer was at a crossroads as World War II came to an end. The success of the Manhattan Project in making the atomic bomb changed the course of history for good, but it also made Oppenheimer think about the right and wrong of what he had done. Oppenheimer felt bad about his role in the bombings of Hiroshima and Nagasaki, which showed how destructive the atomic bomb could be.

In 1947, Oppenheimer's activities after the war took an unexpected turn when he got caught up in the Cold War's politics. During this time, people were more suspicious and worried about communism, especially in the US government. Oppenheimer was investigated because he had worked with left-wing groups in the past. He was called to testify before the Atomic Energy Commission (AEC). Oppenheimer's personal and professional life would be changed forever by this Security Hearing.

Oppenheimer had a hard time at the Security Hearing because he was asked a lot of tough questions about his political views during the war. Oppenheimer was at first seen as a patriotic hero because he helped make the atomic bomb, but his activities and relationships were closely watched. Oppenheimer's reputation was ruined by claims that he was a communist sympathizer and a security risk. This left him alone and removed from his once respected position.

In 1954, when Oppenheimer's security clearance was officially taken away, the Security Hearing reached its peak. The government's decision was based on who he knew in the past and the fact that they thought he was a communist. This decision had huge repercussions for Oppenheimer. He was kicked out of important scientific jobs and banned from contributing to any more government-controlled research.

Even though he had problems, Oppenheimer was still passionate about his work and looked for other ways to stay involved in science. He then turned his attention to promoting education as a key way to make scientific progress. Oppenheimer argued passionately for the need for the government to fund scientific research and invest in the next generation of scientists.

The Institute for Advanced Study (IAS) was started by Oppenheimer in Princeton, New Jersey, in 1947. The IAS was a haven for intellectual pursuits, bringing together smart people from different fields who wanted to work together and push the limits of knowledge. Oppenheimer's job as director of the institute gave him the chance to continue fostering scientific progress, but the Security Hearing continued to hang over his career for a long time.

In the years after his security clearance was taken away, Oppenheimer's personal life was still full of trouble. His health started to get worse, and it was hard for him to keep up with his own research. Scientists still recognized Oppenheimer's contributions and praised his groundbreaking work on the theory of black holes. Even though he wasn't as active in science as he once was, his reputation as one of the best minds of the 20th century stayed the same.

Robert Oppenheimer's life after the war was complicated and affected by the political and social climate of the time. Because he worked on the Manhattan Project, his name will always be linked to the creation of the atomic bomb.

He never took this responsibility lightly. Even though the Security Hearing hurt his reputation and limited what he could do, Oppenheimer's dedication to scientific exploration and support for education will always be remembered in the scientific community. Today, his complicated legacy continues to spark debate and thought about the ethical implications of scientific discoveries and the responsibilities of scientists in the face of social and political problems.

12. The Institute for Advanced Study and Robert Oppenheimer

In the years before World War II, many physicists and mathematicians felt a strong sense of urgency to get away from the tumultuous political scene and focus on pure knowledge instead. One of these safe places was the Institute for Advanced Study (IAS), which became a symbol of intellectual freedom for scientists. And it was under Robert Oppenheimer's direction and leadership that the institute changed into a center for cutting-edge research that broke new ground.

The Institute for Advanced Study was started by a small group of forward-thinking people in the early 1930s. They saw the need for a place that would support rigorous and independent research. Notably, the first director, Abraham Flexner, strongly believed in the power of intellectual freedom and unrestricted exploration. But this vision didn't start to come true until 1933, when Louis Bamberger and his sister Caroline Bamberger Fuld gave money to help make it happen.

Robert Oppenheimer was named director of the IAS in 1947, which set the stage for a time of scientific progress that had never been seen before. Oppenheimer was a very smart theoretical physicist who had just finished leading the Manhattan Project, which was a successful effort that made the first atomic bomb. But his work as head of the IAS was very different from what he did during the war.

With the help of the IAS's Board of Trustees and Oppenheimer's leadership, the institute became a good place for intellectual exploration across many fields. At first, the institute was known for its work in theoretical physics, but Oppenheimer wanted to broaden its focus by bringing in scholars from fields like math, economics, philosophy, and history. The approach allowed people from different fields to work together and share ideas that could change the world.

The success of the institute was largely due to Oppenheimer's commitment to helping the next generation of scientists and scholars. He knew how important it was to teach his students and get them interested in learning more. Both the professors and the graduate students did well in an environment where talking, arguing, and working together were not only encouraged but also expected.

During Oppenheimer's time at the IAS, a lot of smart people joined, and many of them went on to be well-known in their fields. The institute became a place where many different ideas came together, always challenging what was thought to be true and breaking new ground. Some of the most important scientific and mathematical discoveries of the 20th century came about because Oppenheimer and the IAS made it easy for people to work together.

Promoting intellectual freedom was one of the most important things Oppenheimer did as a leader. He thought that groundbreaking ideas often came from thinking outside the box. Because of this, he encouraged academics to push the limits and question existing ideas. This idea became the most important part of the institute's philosophy, and it still guides its research to this day.

Under the direction of Robert Oppenheimer, the Institute for Advanced Study was a safe place for some of the world's smartest people during a time of political turmoil. The institute became a breeding ground for new ideas and paved the way for many scientific breakthroughs, securing its place in intellectual history for all time.

13. The Atomic Energy Commission and Robert Oppenheimer

In the history of nuclear research and development in the United States, the creation of the Atomic Energy Commission (AEC) was a major turning point. This chapter talks about the important role that famous physicist Robert Oppenheimer played as the first chairman of the Atomic Energy Commission (AEC). It also talks about the challenges that both Oppenheimer and the AEC faced when trying to shape the future of atomic energy in the years after World War II.

The Atomic Energy Act of 1946, which was signed into law by President Harry S. Truman on August 1, 1946, was the law that made the Atomic Energy Commission. Its main job was to watch over the development and use of atomic energy for both military and civilian purposes. The act emphasized the need for civilian control over atomic energy and called for the creation of a governing body to guide the country's nuclear efforts.

President Truman chose Robert Oppenheimer, who was a key figure in making the atomic bomb during the Manhattan Project, to be the first head of the AEC. Oppenheimer was an expert in nuclear physics and knew a lot about the scientific and moral consequences of atomic energy. People thought that by putting him in charge, nuclear research and production would be more closely watched and controlled.

As the first leader of the AEC, Oppenheimer had to deal with a lot of problems. One of his main jobs was to find a balance between how atomic energy was used by the military and by civilians. The AEC was in charge of both developing nuclear weapons and promoting peaceful uses of nuclear power. Oppenheimer tried to find a balance between these two goals by pushing for international cooperation on atomic energy and making sure that national security was protected.

Concerns were raised about Oppenheimer's loyalty and how he handled secret information at the beginning of the 1950s. People said he was a Communist because he used to hang out with people who were on the left. The Atomic Energy Commission held a security hearing that got a lot of attention to look into these claims. Even though Oppenheimer helped with the atomic bomb project, he was closely watched at the hearing, and in 1954, his security clearance was taken away.

Oppenheimer's time as the first head of the Atomic Energy Commission changed the field of atomic energy in a way that can't be erased. His vision and leadership made it possible for peaceful uses of nuclear power to grow, such as the building of research reactors and the use of nuclear energy to make electricity. Even though Oppenheimer lost his security clearance, his contributions to atomic energy and his role in making the AEC's policies were still important.

When Robert Oppenheimer was in charge of the Atomic Energy Commission when it was just getting started, it shows how hard it was for both the commission and its leader. Even though his security clearance being taken away caused some controversy, Oppenheimer will always be remembered as a leader in the responsible development and use of atomic energy. Under his leadership, the AEC laid the groundwork for future improvements in nuclear technology and stressed the importance of working with other countries to manage atomic energy.

14. The Security Hearing of Robert Oppenheimer

As the Security Hearing of Robert Oppenheimer, a famous physicist and the man in charge of the Manhattan Project, began, the room was filled with tension. In 1954, the paranoia of the Cold War had gripped the United States. People were questioning how loyal Oppenheimer was to his country, and the stakes couldn't have been higher.

As the hearing started, a group of government officials and security experts sat down in front of Oppenheimer, who was sitting tall and calm. The room was full of people who were excited to hear what was going to happen. It was a fight between science, patriotism, and the temptation of doing something bad.

The hearing was held to find out more about Oppenheimer's security clearance, which he had while the atomic bomb was being made. The government was worried that he might have been a communist sympathizer because of the people he knew and the way he voted in the past. Depending on what happened at this hearing, Oppenheimer would either keep his security clearance or be seen as a security risk.

As soon as the first witness was called, everyone in the room fell silent. Oppenheimer's defense team had worked hard to get ready for this hearing, putting together a group of people who could testify to his loyalty and dedication to the U.S. The witnesses, who were well-known scientists and colleagues, talked about how dedicated Oppenheimer was to the project and how smart he was as a scientist.

But the prosecution was just as determined to show that they were right. They called their own witnesses, people who had worked closely with Oppenheimer and thought that his political views clouded his judgment. These witnesses said that they were worried about other scientists who they thought were communists and that Oppenheimer hadn't done enough to find possible threats.

The hearing turned into a battleground of different testimonies, with both sides bringing evidence to back up their arguments. Oppenheimer's defense team said that his ties to people on the left were just part of his job as a scientist and did not make him less loyal to the United States. The prosecution, on the other hand, pointed to his past words and groups he was a part of as evidence of possible subversion.

The media circus around the hearing grew as the days turned into weeks. Newspapers wrote about every little detail, and people crowded around their radios to hear what happened. With Oppenheimer at its center, the case had become a symbol of the larger struggle between scientific freedom and government control.

After months of hearing witnesses and talking about what they said, a decision was finally made. There were a lot of people in the courtroom when the verdict was read, and you could feel the tension. The panel came to the conclusion that Oppenheimer's connections were troubling, but there was no proof that he was a security risk right away. As a compromise, they suggested that his security clearance be lowered, which would mean he wouldn't be able to see as much classified information.

Oppenheimer felt both happy and sad about what happened after the hearings. Even though his career had been ruined, he was still respected and admired by the scientific community. The experience made him unhappy with how the government treated scientists and how civil liberties were being taken away during the paranoid Cold War.

In the years that followed, Oppenheimer turned his attention to promoting international scientific cooperation and
getting rid of nuclear weapons. His voice would have a big
impact on how nuclear policy was made around the
world, making him an icon in both science and politics.

The Robert Oppenheimer Security Hearing was over, but
its effects would be felt for years to come. It was a story to
teach people a lesson and show how hard it is to keep national security and individual rights in balance. Even
though Oppenheimer's reputation had been hurt, his contributions to science and his influence on world affairs
would always be a testament to his lasting legacy.

15. The Scientific Theories of Robert Oppenheimer

Robert Oppenheimer was a very smart physicist who made a lot of important contributions to theoretical physics and nuclear science. His scientific ideas were very important in making the atomic bomb, and they set the stage for modern nuclear physics. In this chapter, we'll look at some of Oppenheimer's most important scientific ideas, including what they mean and how they changed the world.

Oppenheimer was one of the first people to study quantum mechanics. Quantum mechanics is a branch of physics that looks at how particles behave at the atomic and subatomic levels. He made important contributions to our understanding of quantum field theory, which combines quantum mechanics and special relativity.

The work that Oppenheimer did on quantum mechanics was important to the development of the atomic bomb. His calculations and theories helped scientists learn a lot about how subatomic particles behave and how to use the huge amount of energy that is stored in atomic nuclei.

Oppenheimer and physicist Melba Phillips came up with the Oppenheimer-Phillips process, which is an important way for nuclear fusion reactions to happen. In this process, two nuclei bump into each other and overcome their electrostatic repulsion to make a larger, more stable nucleus.

The Oppenheimer-Phillips process was very important for understanding stellar nucleosynthesis, which is how elements are made inside stars. This theory had important effects on astrophysics and helped us learn more about how the universe is made up and how it has changed over time.

Oppenheimer made important contributions to the field of astrophysics, especially when it came to understanding how massive stars behave and how gravitational collapse works. Oppenheimer and his student Hartland Snyder came up with the Oppenheimer-Snyder model, which explains how black holes and neutron stars are made.

This model said that when a big star runs out of nuclear fuel, it goes supernova and leaves either a black hole or a neutron star behind, depending on how big it was to start with. Oppenheimer's ideas about black holes and neutron stars changed the way we think about these mysterious celestial objects and led to new research in the field of astrophysics.

Oppenheimer did a lot of work in the field of quantum mechanics, which helped him come up with the theory of the bipolar quantum oscillator. This theory describes a system of particles that have both forces that pull them together and forces that push them apart.

Oppenheimer's theory of bipolar quantum oscillators is useful in many areas of physics, such as quantum optics and condensed matter physics. It gave us new information about how quantum systems behave and how they interact, which helped us make things like lasers and superconductors.

The scientific ideas of Robert Oppenheimer have had a lasting effect on nuclear physics, astrophysics, and quantum mechanics. His work on quantum field theory, nuclear fusion, stellar nucleosynthesis, black holes, and quantum oscillators changed the field of physics and led to many new discoveries.

Oppenheimer's scientific ideas were key to making the

atomic bomb, and they also helped us learn more about

the universe and how it works at its most basic level. His

theoretical work continues to inspire scientists today and

in the future, and it shows how powerful the human mind

and scientific curiosity are.

16. The Final Years and the Shadow of Death

Robert Oppenheimer was at a crossroads as the world started a new era after the horrors of World War II. The brilliant physicist, who was once called the "father of the atomic bomb," was now trying to deal with the huge amount of power he had helped bring into the world. This chapter looks at the last few years of Oppenheimer's life, which were filled with personal struggles, political persecution, and the knowledge that his time on earth was coming to an end.

In the years after World War II, there was a lot of public opinion against making and using atomic weapons. Oppenheimer was haunted by how much damage had been done and became a supporter of putting nuclear weapons under international control. He saw nuclear power as a two-sided sword that could both make great progress and cause unimaginable destruction. Because he had been involved with leftist groups when he was younger, this new position put him at odds with the U.S. government. They saw him as a possible security risk.

In 1954, Oppenheimer's life was turned upside down when he was accused of being a security risk and having ties to communist groups. The U.S. Atomic Energy Commission took away his security clearance, which meant he could no longer have a big say in how nuclear policy is made in the U.S. After that, there was a long, hard hearing where Oppenheimer had to defend himself against charges of disloyalty and betrayal. Even though many scientists and intellectuals supported him, Oppenheimer's reputation was hurt, and he was never put back in his old positions of power.

While the political storm was going on, Oppenheimer was also fighting for his health. Oppenheimer had been sick his whole life, but it wasn't until his last few years that they started to hurt him. His breathing problems got worse, and it became clear that he had lung cancer. Even though Oppenheimer's health was getting worse, he didn't let it get him down. He kept writing and giving lectures to help the scientific community. Oppenheimer felt sad when he realized that he was both the man who had destroyed Hiroshima and Nagasaki in ways that had never been done before and the scientist who had used the power of the atom for the good of humanity. He often thought about the right and wrong of what he did, struggling with the weight of the lives lost because of the weapons he helped make.

In the summer of 1967, Oppenheimer began the last part of his life, which he spent with family and friends. He gave in to his love of literature and poetry and found comfort in the verses of the Bhagavad Gita, which he had grown to like while living in the New Mexico desert. Oppenheimer's mind often went to the big questions of existence, life, and death as he tried to find peace with a world that would never be the same again thanks to his work.

Robert Oppenheimer died at his home in Princeton, New Jersey, on February 18, 1967. His fights with the world and his own conscience were finally over. As the scientist who led the Manhattan Project and as the conscience who questioned the effects of technological progress, he left a legacy that continues to shape the course of human history. Oppenheimer's life is a stark reminder of how morality and power are intertwined, and his last years show how hard it was for a flawed genius to figure out where he fit in a world with huge consequences.

17. The Enduring Legacy of Robert Oppenheimer

Robert Oppenheimer, who is often called the "Father of the Atomic Bomb," left behind a rich and complicated legacy that continues to shape science, politics, and ethics in the modern world. As we look into the effects of his work and the problems in his personal life, we find both praise and criticism for a scientist whose work changed the course of history for good. This chapter looks at Robert Oppenheimer's lasting legacy by looking at what he did, what happened because of what he did, and the ongoing debates about his character.

The most important things Robert Oppenheimer did were make scientific breakthroughs and lead the Manhattan Project. As the scientific director, Oppenheimer was able to get some of the best nuclear physicists to work together to create a weapon that could use the huge power of nuclear fission. His charisma and intelligence were very important in coordinating the huge scientific effort that led to the creation and successful testing of the first atomic bomb and the start of the nuclear age.

Even though Oppenheimer did important things in the field of nuclear science, his legacy is also tied to a moral question. Seeing the atomic bomb destroy Hiroshima and Nagasaki in a way that had never been done before made Oppenheimer think deeply about what was right and wrong. He became a strong supporter of international control and peaceful use of nuclear energy. He was worried about the spread of nuclear weapons without being stopped.

But Oppenheimer's change of stance to support getting rid of nuclear weapons caused political tension and mistrust.

In 1954, at the height of the Cold War, he had to go to a security clearance hearing where his loyalty to the United States was questioned because he had worked with people who were left-leaning or communist in the past. The trial showed the internal conflict between protecting national security and Oppenheimer's commitment to openness, freedom of thought, and working with people from other countries. Even though Oppenheimer was found not guilty of disloyalty, the trial hurt his reputation and made it harder for him to get jobs in the future.

In the past few years, people have thought more and more about Oppenheimer's legacy and how the trial affected his reputation. Critics say that the government's decision to take away his security clearance because Oppenheimer had moral doubts about using nuclear weapons was unfair. Many people think he should be honored for his work in science and for trying to stop the nuclear arms race after that.

In addition to his work on the Manhattan Project, Oppenheimer was a key figure in shaping scientific education and research. He was the head of the Institute for Advanced Study in Princeton, and he was a mentor to a whole generation of physicists. Oppenheimer's dedication to interdisciplinary studies, scientific exploration, and intellectual freedom left an indelible mark on the academic world, creating an atmosphere of collaboration and intellectual rigor.

In the end, Robert Oppenheimer's legacy is one of deep ethical questions about scientific discovery and its possible consequences. He reminds us that scientific progress must go hand in hand with careful thought, accountability, and a commitment to the well-being of all people.

Oppenheimer's legacy keeps pushing scientists, policy-makers, and activists to think about the ethical aspects of scientific progress and make sure that knowledge is used in a responsible way.

Robert Oppenheimer's lasting legacy includes his great scientific work, the moral questions he had to deal with, and the controversies that surrounded his personal and political life. He left his mark on the world through his work in nuclear science and his efforts to get people to use scientific knowledge in a responsible way. As we think about Robert Oppenheimer's complicated legacy, we are reminded that science and ethics must work together to lead us to a future in which the benefits of scientific progress are used for the good of all people.

18. The Key Factors to Robert Oppenheimer's Success

Robert Oppenheimer was one of the most famous physicists of the 20th century. During World War II, he was a key part of the team that made the atomic bomb. His success was not just a matter of luck. Instead, it was a result of a number of important things that helped him reach the top of his field. In this chapter, we'll talk about the things that led to Oppenheimer's success and made him an important figure in science. One of the main reasons Robert Oppenheimer was so successful was that he had a great education. Oppenheimer was born into a wealthy family, so he was able to go to well-known schools like Harvard University, where he studied chemistry, and the University of Gottingen in Germany, where he got his Ph.D. in physics. His strong academic background set him up to be successful in the field of physics in the future.

Oppenheimer's success was largely due to his brilliant mind and intellectual curiosity. Throughout his career, he showed an insatiable desire to learn and a deep-seated desire to figure out how the universe works. He was able to make important breakthroughs in theoretical physics and atomic research because he could think creatively, ask deep questions, and connect different areas of knowledge.

Oppenheimer was a great leader and was very good at getting things done. These skills were crucial to the success of the Manhattan Project. As the scientific director of the project, he had the difficult job of leading a group of smart people and making sure they worked well together and stuck to strict deadlines. He was an excellent leader because he knew how to delegate tasks well, make people feel like they were all in it together, and handle complicated projects. Part of Oppenheimer's success was also due to the large number of connections and collaborations he had in the scientific community. He actively looked for partnerships with the best scientists and thinkers, with whom he could share ideas and work to advance science. This network gave him access to useful resources, helped him get money for his research, and brought attention to his ground-breaking work.

Oppenheimer's success was in large part due to his love of teaching and mentoring. Even though he had a lot of research to do, he took time to teach and guide young physicists. He helped them reach their full potential and encouraged them to push the limits of scientific inquiry. Through his teaching, Oppenheimer left a legacy that continues to inspire scientists today.

Even though Oppenheimer's role in making the atomic bomb was controversial, he was successful in part because he had a strong sense of right and wrong and a moral compass. After seeing how the bomb destroyed Hiroshima and Nagasaki, Oppenheimer became a strong supporter of arms control and disarmament. This stood him in good stead and cemented his reputation as a scientist who thought about the moral implications of his work.

Robert Oppenheimer's success was due to a unique set of circumstances that propelled him to the top of the scientific world. His excellent education, intellectual brilliance, leadership skills, ability to make connections, love of teaching, and strong sense of ethics helped him get where he is today. Not only did Oppenheimer's work change the field of physics, but it also changed the course of history. His amazing story is an inspiration for people who want to be scientists, and it shows the key things that can lead to success in any field.

19. The Key Factors of Failure - Robert Oppenheimer

Robert Oppenheimer was one of the smartest scientists of the 20th century. During World War II, he was a key part of the team that made the atomic bomb. He was charming, smart, and had an intelligence that was unmatched. Even though Oppenheimer had a lot of great qualities, he ended up failing because of a number of important things. In this chapter, we'll look more closely at these things and talk about how they led to Oppenheimer's failure.

Political interference was one of the main reasons why Oppenheimer failed. In the 1950s, the United States government went on a witch hunt against people who were thought to be communists. Oppenheimer was an easy target because he had worked with left-wing intellectuals in the past and held liberal views. After a very controversial hearing, his security clearance was eventually taken away. This ended his role in the scientific community and ruined his career.

Another important reason for Oppenheimer's failure was that he had trouble getting along with key people in the scientific community. Some of Oppenheimer's coworkers didn't like his way of managing and personality, which led to bad feelings and disagreements at work. This tension made it hard to get projects done smoothly and made the work environment bad, which could have affected the results of his efforts.

When Oppenheimer worked on making the atomic bomb, he faced moral problems that followed him for the rest of his life. As the head of the Manhattan Project, he had to decide whether or not to use the huge destructive power he had helped make. Oppenheimer struggled with this problem and spoke out against making more hydrogen bombs. This put him at odds with the military-industrial complex and other powerful parts of the government.

After World War II ended, Oppenheimer's influence started to decrease. As the Cold War got worse, nuclear technology was used more and more for military purposes, and the focus moved away from scientific discovery and toward strategic development. Oppenheimer's nuclear vision, which was based on international cooperation and limiting the number of weapons, became less important as tensions between the US and the USSR grew. This loss of power made it harder for him to change policy, which led to his eventual failure.

Even though Oppenheimer was very smart, he had some personality flaws that hurt him and led to his failure. People said he was hard to decide on things and often doubted himself. These things made it hard for him to make decisions, which led to delays and missed chances. The public's view of Oppenheimer was also hurt by his reputation as a womanizer and by his questionable personal choices. This made him an easy target for people who wanted to undermine his authority.

Robert Oppenheimer's failure can be traced back to a number of complex and interconnected key factors. Political meddling, strained relationships, moral dilemmas, losing power, and his own flaws all played a big part in his downfall. Even though he made a lot of important contributions to science, Oppenheimer's career eventually went downhill because of these things. His story is a warning about how even the smartest people can lose their way because of things they can't change.

20. Oppenheimer's Agonizing Decision

On August 9, 1945, just three days after the horrifying destruction of Hiroshima, the United States dropped an atomic bomb on the city of Nagasaki. This was a terrible turning point in history. When Robert Oppenheimer, who was in charge of the scientific side of the Manhattan Project, realized how much damage and loss of innocent lives these bombs would cause, he had to deal with a complicated mix of emotions, morals, and the weight of responsibility.

As Oppenheimer stood by the window of his office in Los Alamos, New Mexico, he couldn't get rid of the pain in his heart. The goal of the project he had been in charge of was to end the bloody war that had spread around the world, but what happened was much worse than he had ever imagined. The bombings were a turning point in his life, and he will always be remembered as the "father of the atomic bomb."

His mind kept going back to the morning of July 16, 1945, when the first test of their invention, which they called "Trinity," took place in the desert of New Mexico. It was a terrible day. As the bomb exploded with such force that it shook the earth, Oppenheimer felt a deep sense of dread. The blinding light, the deafening noise, and the huge amount of power that was released were too much to handle. Later, Oppenheimer famously used a quote from Hindu scripture to call it a "destroyer of worlds."

Now that Hiroshima and Nagasaki were real, Oppenheimer couldn't get rid of the haunting images that kept coming into his mind. The news stories that got to him told of unimaginable pain and destruction. In the blink of an eye, hundreds of people died, their ghostly shadows were burned into the walls, and the whole city was turned into rubble. Justice had been done, but it had come at a terrible price.

Oppenheimer's morals revolted when he saw a lot of innocent civilians being killed. Everything about his sense of right and wrong screamed at him. As a scientist with big ideas, he was amazed by how powerful the atomic bomb was and how much it could do. But seeing the terrible results broke his illusion that war could be controlled. The weapon they made was too strong and could kill anyone. It wasn't a surgical tool, but a powerful force that changed what it meant to be human.

His heart hurt as he thought about all the broken families, children taken from their homes, and lives that would never be the same again. The weight of his job as the scientific director of the Manhattan Project, which had seemed like a necessary sacrifice to end the war, was now heavy on his soul. Had anyone really thought about how powerful this weapon could be?

Oppenheimer felt better when he was alone in his office. He thought about the choices and decisions that had led up to this moment, the race against time to make a weapon to stop Nazi Germany's plans. Science used to seem like the answer, but now he wondered about its darker side. The terrible things that happened in Hiroshima and Nagasaki forced him to think about the power and ethics of his life's work. As the days turned into weeks, Oppenheimer got deeper and deeper into an inner struggle, trying to figure out what was right and wrong. He realized that he couldn't just say that he wasn't responsible for the damage he caused. With equal parts regret and determination, Oppenheimer knew that it was his job to make sure that people learned from the atomic bomb's terrible failures and atrocities.

Robert Oppenheimer became a strong supporter of disarmament and nuclear control in the years that followed. He worked hard to get international agreements to stop the spread and use of atomic weapons. He did this because he was very aware of the moral weight of his role in the Manhattan Project.

The bombings of Hiroshima and Nagasaki shook the world to its core. They changed the course of history and the way people think about wars in a way that will never be undone. Robert Oppenheimer would always be haunted by the images and feelings connected to these events, but he turned his pain into a relentless quest to make sure that the atomic bomb's legacy would be a force for peace instead of a sign of destruction.

21. The Atomic Spies of Robert Oppenheimer

The United States was in a race against time to make an atomic bomb during World War II. In this high-pressure situation, the Manhattan Project was started, which brought together some of the best scientists and engineers. Robert Oppenheimer, a brilliant physicist who became known as the "father of the atomic bomb," was in charge of this project. But in the shadows was a group of people who would later be called the atomic spies.

Oppenheimer didn't know that spies were working on his project because he was so focused on the huge task at hand. The most important thing to him was to finish building the atomic bomb before the enemy did. There was a lot of secrecy around the project, and only a few people were trusted to know that it existed, let alone what it was about.

Unfortunately, this gave a network of spies a chance to get into the project's ranks.

Klaus Fuchs, a British physicist who was born in Germany, was one of the most well-known atomic spies. In 1944, Fuchs became part of the British Mission at Los Alamos. Since the late 1930s, he had been sending secret information to the Soviet Union without anyone else knowing. Fuchs was driven by his belief in communism, which led him to see the Soviet Union as a partner in the fight against fascism. His knowledge of the plans and progress of the Manhattan Project was very helpful to the Soviets and sped up their own atomic research.

At the same time, David Greenglass, another atomic spy, was working closer to home. Greenglass was an American who worked as a machinist at Los Alamos. Julius Rosenberg, who was Greenglass's brother-in-law, had asked him to join. In exchange for money, Greenglass gave over sketches and written descriptions of the device used in the atomic bomb to make it explode. Because Rosenberg knew a lot of people, this information got to Soviet intelligence. The Soviets used Greenglass as a key source of information that helped them learn more about how the American atomic bomb worked.

How much the atomic spies did would not be known until after the war was over. In 1949, British intelligence found evidence of spying and was able to link it to Fuchs. Faced with a lot of evidence, Fuchs admitted what he had done and was sentenced to 14 years in prison. When Fuchs's betrayal became public, it led to a big investigation in the United States. This led to the arrest of Julius and Ethel Rosenberg, who were later found guilty of espionage and put to death in 1953.

The atomic spies had a big effect on how the atomic bomb was made and how the world worked after the war. Their actions not only helped the Soviet Union get closer to building atomic weapons, but they also made things worse between the US and its allies as the Cold War began.

When Robert Oppenheimer found out that spies had messed with his project, it was a huge blow. Even though Oppenheimer had a high level of security clearance and trusted his team, he had no idea what the atomic spies were doing. The incident showed that even the most secret projects are vulnerable and made people wonder how well security protocols work.

As the war ended and the world tried to figure out how to deal with the effects of the atomic bomb, the atomic spies became less well-known. Even though their actions changed history, in the end they were just small parts of the bigger story of the atomic age. Still, the chapter they wrote would always be a reminder of how dangerous espionage is and how important it is to keep sensitive information safe.

22. The Interim Committee and Robert Oppenheimer's Role

As the Manhattan Project moved forward, it was clear that decisions about how and where the atomic bomb would be used needed to be made at a higher level. In April 1945, President Harry S. Truman put together the Interim Committee, which was made up of powerful people who were supposed to give him advice on nuclear issues.

The Interim Committee was made up of well-known scientists, military officials, and policymakers who had the knowledge and power to figure out what would happen if atomic weapons were used.

Dr. Vannevar Bush, Secretary of State James F. Byrnes, and economist and diplomat John J. McCloy were all on the committee, which was led by Secretary of War Henry L. Stimson.

Dr. J. Robert Oppenheimer, who was known as the scientific leader of the Manhattan Project, was an important member of the Interim Committee. Oppenheimer's work on the project and his knowledge of what the bomb could do made him an extremely valuable member of the committee.

Oppenheimer was in charge of the Los Alamos Laboratory, which was a key part of the team that made the atomic bomb. Because of how smart he was in science and how well he understood the technical parts of the project, he had a lot of power on the Interim Committee.

Oppenheimer was a respected member of the committee because he knew a lot about nuclear physics and was concerned about the moral effects of atomic weapons. Because of his knowledge, he was able to give important information about the science and technology behind the bomb, which helped the committee figure out how it could be used.

The Interim Committee had a hard job: they had to tell President Truman whether or not to use the atomic bomb on Japan and, if they did, how to do it. They knew that the bomb could do a lot of damage and that it would be wrong to use it.

Oppenheimer's ideas were very important to these talks. He asked the committee to think about how the bomb would affect civilians, saying that a test could convince Japan to give up without having to use it right away. But military issues, like the need to end the war quickly, were also very important to the talks.

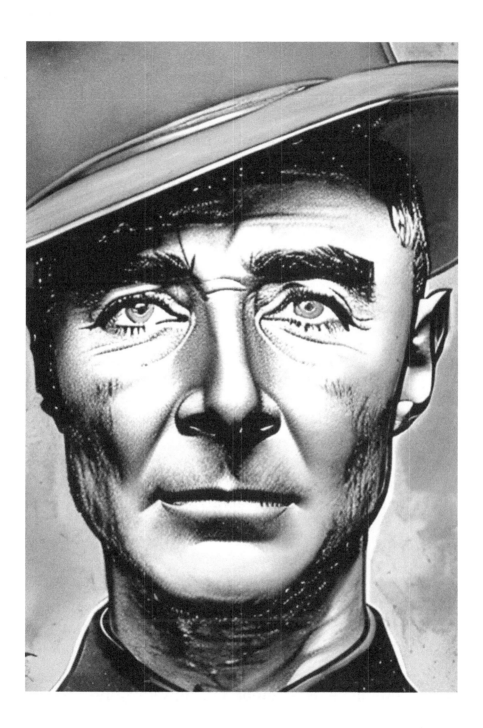

In June 1945, the Interim Committee told President Truman that the atomic bomb should be used against Japan. They emphasized the bomb's immediate military advantage and the fact that it could save millions of lives that could have been lost in an invasion of Japan. The committee also said that a demonstration test should be done if Japan doesn't give up.

Oppenheimer believed that the atomic bomb should be used, but he had some doubts about it. Even though he knew it was important to end the war quickly, he also knew that using nuclear weapons could have terrible effects on the future of humanity.

Even with these moral problems, Oppenheimer saw that the war was real and that the recommendations of the Interim Committee were important. As a scientific advisor, he thought carefully about the possible outcomes and tried to make the best choice based on the information he had.

The Interim Committee was a very important group of smart people and influential people who helped make decisions about how to use the atomic bomb. Robert Oppenheimer's scientific knowledge, moral sense, and respect within the committee gave him a lot to add to the discussions and helped shape the recommendations made by the committee.

In the end, President Truman decided to drop atomic bombs on Hiroshima and Nagasaki because of what the Interim Committee said. The decision and Oppenheimer's part in it would have long-lasting effects and spark debates about the right way to use nuclear weapons.

23. A Contentious Relationship: Lewis Strauss and Robert Oppenheimer

This chapter goes into detail about how hard it was for Lewis Strauss and Robert Oppenheimer to get along. Both of these men were very important to the development of nuclear weapons and the US atomic energy program as a whole. But a series of events and philosophical differences made them very angry at each other. This chapter looks at what went wrong in their relationship and how that affected their careers.

The chapter starts by looking at Oppenheimer's meteoric rise in the scientific world and his important role as the scientific director of the Manhattan Project during World War II. It shows that Oppenheimer was a key figure in the development of the atomic bomb and other nuclear advances because of how smart and visionary he was as a leader.

The story then moves on to talk about Lewis Strauss, a smart businessman and influential political figure. Strauss got important jobs because of his knowledge of energy and his connections in the Republican Party. He became Chairman of the Atomic Energy Commission (AEC), for example. The chapter looks at his strong belief that nuclear power could be used for both military and business purposes.

This part looks at how the two men's personalities and backgrounds are different. Oppenheimer was a smart and talented physicist who took a more liberal view of nuclear power and pushed for international cooperation and control. Strauss, on the other hand, with his business background, stressed the importance of a strong defense and a limited policy of sharing nuclear weapons.

The main disagreement between the two men happened in 1954, when Oppenheimer went to court to get a security clearance. Strauss, who is now Chairman of the AEC, led the effort to get Oppenheimer's clearance taken away because of worries about his communist sympathies and his opposition to making the hydrogen bomb. This section gives a detailed look at the hearings, including the people who testified and the decision to take away Oppenheimer's clearance.

The chapter goes on to look at the effects of Oppenheimer's clearance being taken away, including how it affected his career and reputation. It shows how angry people were and how this led to debates. It also talks about Strauss's role in promoting the idea of fallout shelters as a way to protect people from possible nuclear attacks, which was a very controversial idea at the time.

This part shows how Oppenheimer's reputation in the scientific world was able to be fixed over time. It talks about how people have recognized his important contributions to nuclear physics, how he has won prestigious awards, and how he has been an important scientific advisor.

The last part of the chapter looks at Strauss's troubled legacy. Even though he was successful in moving the nuclear energy program forward and had a lot of power in the Eisenhower administration, he was criticized for being rude to Oppenheimer and how he handled the clearance hearings. Strauss's reputation took a hit, which made his other accomplishments less impressive.

At the end of the chapter, we think about how Strauss and Oppenheimer's tense relationship still affects us today. It shows how important their different ideas about nuclear power and their different roles in the atomic energy program are. In the end, this chapter tries to explain how complicated their relationship was and how it changed the nuclear situation in the United States.

24. Oppenheimer (Film): A Tragic Genius Unveiled

As the bright lights of Los Angeles went out and the theater curtain slowly went up, the audience was taken to a different time and place. They were about to go on a trip that would change the way they thought about one of the smartest scientists in history for good. The projector started up with a flicker, casting an ethereal glow over the eager faces and announcing the start of an interesting story: "Oppenheimer."

"Oppenheimer," which was directed by the well-known filmmaker Robert Wilson, tried to show J. Robert Oppenheimer's amazing life and deeply complicated personality. In this chapter, we go deeper into Wilson's story and look at the key moments and emotional complexities that were shown on the big screen.

In the beginning of the movie, a young, brilliant student named Robert Oppenheimer is struggling with existential questions that will shape his life. Robert grew up in a liberal Jewish family, where he showed early signs of intellectual curiosity, a strong desire to learn, and a sharp mind. Wilson does a great job of capturing these formative years by giving them a feeling of intellectual ferment and cultural change.

As the story goes on, the audience is taken back to when Oppenheimer was at the University of Cambridge, where he was a part of a lively scientific community. Wilson does a beautiful job of showing the heated debates about quantum mechanics, the rise of fascism, and the threat of war, all of which put Oppenheimer's core beliefs to the test and made him even more committed to science as a force for good.

The movie shows how important Oppenheimer's role was in the top-secret Manhattan Project, which used the power of atomic energy to make the world's first atomic bomb. Wilson does a great job of showing Oppenheimer's moral problems by putting his scientific achievements next to the terrible effects of his invention. The audience sees Oppenheimer's growing unease as he struggles with the size of what he has made and wonders about the moral implications and his own responsibility.

As the Second World War comes to an end, Oppenheimer can't get over how shocking and terrible it was to drop atomic bombs on Hiroshima and Nagasaki. His inner turmoil comes out in haunting monologues that show the audience the weight he's carrying. Wilson does a good job of showing how heavy the nuclear age is, bringing to life Oppenheimer's famous quote from Albert Camus: "Now we are all sons of bitches."

The film ends with Oppenheimer's troubled life during the Red Scare, when he was accused of having communist sympathies and had his security clearance taken away. Wilson does a great job of showing how paranoia and the loss of personal freedoms led to Oppenheimer's tragic downfall, which was caused by political schemes. The audience sees Oppenheimer's inner demons as he faces the results of his actions and sees his lifelong goals fall apart in front of him.

Wilson does a great job of showing the contradiction of a scientific genius who is haunted by the thing he made. The movie does a great job of showing Oppenheimer's complicated personality and the moral problems he had to deal with. This forces the audience to deal with the uncomfortable combination of intellectual brilliance and deep moral responsibility.

As the movie ends and the lights slowly come on, the audience is left to think about the legacy of a man whose contributions to science changed the course of human history for good. Through the lens of Robert Wilson's movie "Oppenheimer," we are reminded that the pursuit of knowledge has consequences and that our lives are a tapestry made up of the choices we make.

25. The Extraordinary Awards of Robert Oppenheimer

Robert Oppenheimer was a well-known physicist and one of the key people who helped make the atomic bomb during World War II. He did a lot of important intellectual and scientific work in his life. Oppenheimer won a lot of awards and honors over the course of his career. This was due to the important work he did in the field of nuclear physics. This chapter will talk about some of the unique awards that Oppenheimer won for his outstanding scientific work.

Soon after World War II ended in 1945, Oppenheimer was one of the top candidates for the Nobel Prize in Physics because of how well he led the Manhattan Project. The prize would have shown how important he was in getting atomic power to work. Even though he never won the

Nobel Prize, the fact that he was nominated for it says a lot about how respected he was in the scientific community.

President Harry S. Truman gave Oppenheimer the Medal for Merit one year after the end of the war. This prestigious civilian award was given to him because of the great things he did for the country during the war. Oppenheimer's tireless work in the race to make the atomic bomb played a big part in how the war turned out, which is why he was given this prestigious award.

In honor of the well-known physicist Enrico Fermi, the United States Atomic Energy Commission made the Enrico Fermi Award. Oppenheimer was the first person to win this prestigious award, which is given for outstanding scientific work. The award showed how Oppenheimer kept making scientific advances in the field of nuclear physics and how he had a long-lasting effect on the peaceful use of atomic energy.

In 1963, Oppenheimer was given the Franklin Medal in Physics by the Franklin Institute, which is known for its dedication to scientific progress. This honor was given to him because of his important contributions to the development of atomic energy, especially his theoretical work in the field of quantum mechanics and his key role in the Manhattan Project.

The Atomic Pioneers Award was given to Oppenheimer after he had worked on the atomic bomb for many years. This award is a reminder of how important he was to the development and regulation of atomic energy. The award showed how much he cared about making sure that nuclear power was used in a safe way and how much he cared about world peace and security.

During his career, Robert Oppenheimer got many more

awards and honorary degrees from respected institutions all over the world. This shows how much of an impact he had on the world of scientific research. Even though the awards mentioned in this chapter give a glimpse into Oppenheimer's amazing life, they are only a small part of the deep and lasting praise he got for his amazing contributions to the field of nuclear physics.

26. The Thesis of Robert Oppenheimer: Bridging Science and Society

We will look at the famous physicist Robert Oppenheimer's thesis and see how he tried to connect science and society. Oppenheimer's thesis was about how scientific discoveries affect society and ethics, especially in light of his work on the Manhattan Project during World War II. This chapter will talk about Oppenheimer's ideas about the responsibility of scientists, his ideas about how nuclear energy can be used peacefully, and the controversy surrounding his political views.

Oppenheimer was sure that scientists had a moral obligation to think about the possible results and ethical problems of their work. His thesis said that the development of atomic weapons during the war showed how much power scientists had and that the scientific community needed to think more about itself. Oppenheimer knew that un-checked scientific progress could have terrible results. He said this to show how important it is to think about ethics when doing science.

In his thesis, Oppenheimer looked at the huge ethical re-sponsibility nuclear scientists have. As the man who in-vented the atomic bomb, he knew what it meant to make such a dangerous weapon. In his thesis, Oppenheimer ar-gued that nuclear scientists had a responsibility to use their knowledge to stop the spread of nuclear weapons and work toward disarmament. He pushed for interna-tional cooperation, treaties, and strict rules to stop the use of nuclear weapons. He also stressed the need for scientists to do their part to make the world safer and more peaceful.

Oppenheimer's ideas about nuclear energy included ways to use it for good, not just for making weapons. In his thesis, he suggested making use of nuclear energy for things like making electricity and making scientific research better. Oppenheimer thought that using the power of atomic energy could do a lot of good for society, as long as it was managed well and shared with people all over the world. He said that scientists should keep working to improve nuclear technology for peaceful and helpful uses and should not use it for destructive purposes.

During the Cold War, Oppenheimer's political views were closely looked at, even though he made many important contributions to science. As a young man, he was a member of the Communist Party, and he was friends with intellectuals who were on the left. This made government agencies suspicious of him. In his thesis, he talked about the tension between science and politics. He showed how hard it was for scientists when their political beliefs were called into question and how that could affect their careers.

Robert Oppenheimer's thesis was about how important it is for scientists to think about the moral implications of their work and to be involved in societal issues. His thesis was a thought-provoking look at how science and society interact. It was about the moral responsibility of nuclear scientists, his ideas for peaceful nuclear energy programs, and the controversy surrounding his political views. By looking at Oppenheimer's point of view, we can learn a lot about how scientists can help shape a better and more moral future for people.

27. The Mentorship of Robert Oppenheimer: Shaping Doctoral Students' Paths to Success

The famous physicist J. Robert Oppenheimer was not only important in making the atomic bomb, but he was also a key figure in training and guiding the scientists of the future. This chapter looks at how Oppenheimer helped his doctoral students learn from his experiences, how they affected him, and how he was a great mentor. Through his unique way of teaching, Oppenheimer left an indelible mark on the scientific community. He changed the paths of his students and helped them do groundbreaking research, become leaders, and become known around the world.

This section is about Robert Oppenheimer's legacy. It talks about his great scientific work, his leadership roles, and how much he changed the world of physics. It looks into why he is so appealing to young scientists who want to get their doctoral degrees as a mentor.

Here, we look at the way of thinking and the philosophy that drove Oppenheimer's ways of mentoring. Using personal stories, interviews, and historical records, this section shows how he encouraged intellectual exploration, fostered collaboration, taught discipline, and encouraged his doctoral students to act in an ethical way.

In this section, we look at Oppenheimer's careful process for choosing doctoral students. It looks at his requirements, his preferences, and the qualities he was looking for in candidates. It also looks at the collaborative and cross-disciplinary nature of research in his group, showing how important it is to work as a team and make intellectual progress   together.

This part goes into detail about how Oppenheimer and his

doctoral students worked together. It talks about how easy it is to reach him, how he helps, and how he gives each student individual attention based on their strengths and goals. In interviews, former students talk about what it was like to have Oppenheimer as a teacher and advisor.

In this section, we talk about how Oppenheimer helped his students become smart scientists. It talks about how he developed critical thinking, creative problem-solving skills, and a deep respect for basic ideas. It also looks at how Oppenheimer inspired and motivated his students to push the limits of science.

This section looks at the effect that Oppenheimer's mentoring had on the careers and scientific contributions of his doctoral students. It shows how his students made important scientific advances in many different ways and fields, leading to faculty positions, leadership roles, and

Nobel Prizes.

At the end of the chapter, we look at how Oppenheimer's mentoring affected his students' views on mentoring and scientific leadership. It looks at how his students went on to become influential mentors who passed on Oppenheimer's philosophy and values to new generations of scientists.

Robert Oppenheimer's work as a mentor to doctoral students changed the way science would be done in the future. His unique ways of teaching, guiding, and helping his students led them to do amazing things and paved the way for scientific breakthroughs that are still having an effect on our world today. The chapter focuses on Oppenheimer's lasting legacy and the huge impact he had on the academic and scientific worlds through his work as a mentor to many outstanding doctoral candidates.

Conclusion

In the end, this book is a fascinating biography that both kids and adults will enjoy. It tells the whole story of Oppenheimer's life, from his childhood to his key role in making the atomic bomb, in an easy-to-understand way that is both interesting and thought-provoking.

By focusing on his complicated personality and his contributions to science, readers learn more about the man who made the bomb and how he changed the world for good. This biography not only teaches and entertains, but also serves as a strong reminder of the moral problems that come up when scientists try to make progress.

Made in the USA
Las Vegas, NV
16 January 2024

84436231R00090